Bannockburn School Dist. 106
2165 Telegraph Road
Bannockburn, Illinois 60015

W9-BJD-574

honey*bees*

BY **Deborah Heiligman**   ILLUSTRATED BY **Carla Golembe**

NATIONAL GEOGRAPHIC SOCIETY
WASHINGTON, D.C.

For my sister worker bees,
The Bucks County Authors of Books for Children:
Laurie Anderson, Liz Bennett, Pat Brisson,
Martha Hewson, Pamela Jane, Sally Keehn,
Susan Korman, Joyce McDonald, Wendy Pfeffer,
Kay Winters, and Elvira Woodruff.
~DH

To my honey, Joe.
~CG

When you see a bee on a warm summer day, do you think, "**Ow!** That bee is going to sting me"?

Don't worry. If that bee is a honeybee, she is after something sweeter than you. She wants nectar, the sweet syrup she finds in flowers. All you have to do is stay out of her way.

Have you ever heard the saying "busy as a bee"? That's about honeybees. There are many kinds of bees, but honeybees are the ones who work really hard—to make honey. In spring and summer, honeybees work about eight hours a day. Some work at night. Most of the bees in a honeybee colony are even called worker bees. And each worker has many jobs in her lifetime.

apple blossom

orange
blossom

dandelion

6

This bee is a worker bee. Right now her job is to collect nectar and bring it back to her colony. The nectar will be made into honey.

But this is not her first job. She has had **many jobs,** and she is only **three weeks old**.

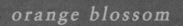

clover

apple blossom

7

Our bee's life began when the queen bee laid a pearly white egg the size of a pinhead. There is only one queen in every bee colony. She is the bee who lays eggs. Each day in spring and summer she lays about 1,500 eggs. She lays the eggs in little rooms called cells.

Most of these eggs become worker bees, like our bee. They are all female. Other eggs become males, or drones. A drone's only job is to mate with the queen. He does no other work at all.

Our bee comes out
of her egg
as a larva.

She stays
in her
little
cell.

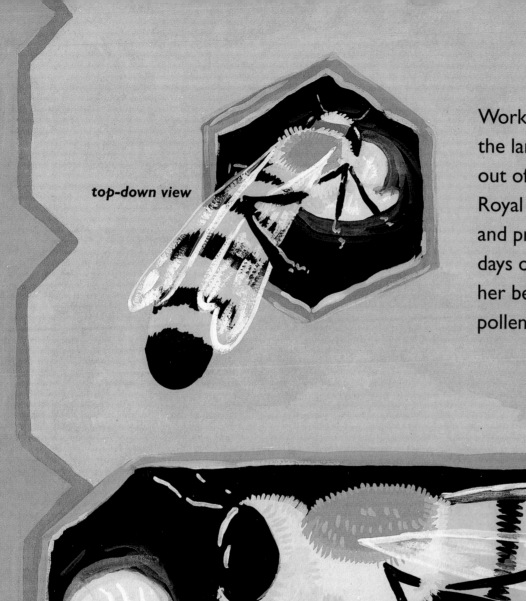

top-down view

side view

Worker bees called nurse bees feed the larva royal jelly, which comes out of glands in a worker bee's head. Royal jelly is packed with vitamins and proteins. When the larva is three days old, the workers begin feeding her beebread, a mixture of honey and pollen from flowers.

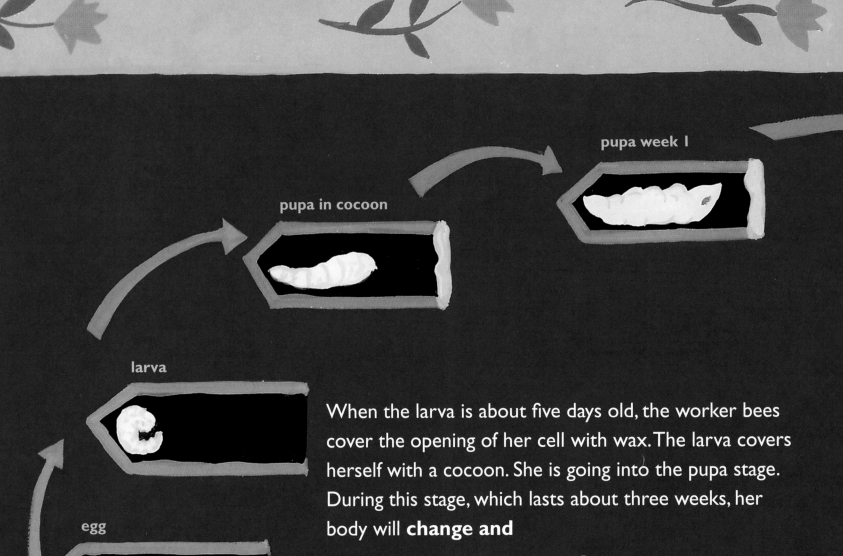

pupa week 1

pupa in cocoon

larva

egg

When the larva is about five days old, the worker bees cover the opening of her cell with wax. The larva covers herself with a cocoon. She is going into the pupa stage. During this stage, which lasts about three weeks, her body will **change and**

change and

change until she is a . . .

pupa week 2

pupa week 3

... grown-up bee!

The first thing she does is bite her way through the wax
and out of her cell. Then she cleans herself up.

Our young worker bee's first job is to clean. Bees don't like any kind of mess. And the queen bee will not lay eggs in a dirty cell. So young worker bees clean out leftover pieces of cocoon, wax, and dirt from the empty cells. Guess how they get rid of all that stuff. They eat it! Then they polish the cell. It takes from 15 to 30 worker bees about 40 minutes to clean and polish each cell. That's all our bee does for the first three days of her life—

clean, clean, clean!

Her next job is to feed the larvae, just as worker bees fed her.
Nurse bees not only feed the larvae, they also check up on them.
They check on each larva more than a thousand times a day.

(Are you OK? Are you OK? Are you OK?)

Beeswax is used in making:

crayons

fake fruit

lipstick

Soon our bee's body starts making wax. Have you heard of beeswax? It comes out of glands in a bee's abdomen. Using the wax, she and her sisters build cells. In some of those cells the queen bee will lay eggs. In other cells the worker bees will store honey. **This is called the honeycomb.** The bees make sure the cells are tilted so the honey won't drip out. Now our bee is called a house bee. House bees fix broken parts of the hive and take care of the queen.

fake fruit

crayons

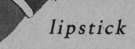
lipstick

crayons

fake fruit

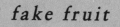
candles

The worker bees feed the queen, groom her, and even carry away her waste. When the hive gets too hot, lots of worker bees gather near the queen and flap their wings to cool her off.

fake fruit

crayons

Soon the worker bee doesn't make as much wax.
Her main job now is to help unload the nectar
older worker bees bring back to the hive. She will eat
some of it and store the rest in honey cells.

To get the nectar, she has to beg for it from the older bees.

A beehive is completely dark, so bees communicate through touch. To beg for nectar, our worker bee drums her antennae on the antennae of a bee who has been out gathering nectar. At the same time she sticks her tongue into the bee's mouth.

The bee who has been gathering nectar has stored it in her honey stomach, which is separate from her other stomach. She now regurgitates, or throws up, the nectar into the beggar's mouth.

Bees use every part of their bodies to do their work—to take care of each other, to make honey, to communicate, to fly, and to guard the hive.

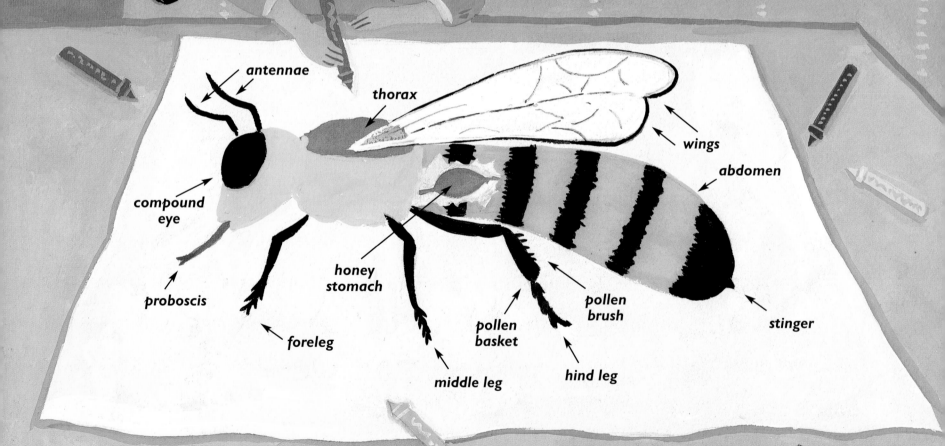

antennae

thorax

wings

abdomen

compound eye

proboscis

honey stomach

pollen basket

pollen brush

stinger

foreleg

middle leg

hind leg

robber bees!

robber bees!

When the worker bee is a little more than two weeks old, she becomes a guard bee. She places herself at the entrance of the hive with other guards. They raise their heads and forelegs. They look ready for anything. And they have to be! The guards' job is to protect the colony from wasps, ants, birds, and mammals, such as bears. But their worst enemies are honeybees from other hives who try to steal their honey. They are called robber bees. These thieves fly back and forth in front of the entrance looking for a chance to slip by the guards.

How can the guard bees tell these bees are not from their hive? They smell different. Bees in a colony pass the queen's smell and taste around when they pass food from bee to bee. So all the bees in one colony smell alike.

Sometimes guard bees need help fighting off intruders, especially big ones like bears. So the guards send out a signal through a special smell. Bees from all over the hive smell the signal and come to help.

Bees usually just chase away intruders. But sometimes they have to sting them. If a bee stings another insect, nothing bad happens to the bee. But if a bee stings a mammal, such as a bear or a dog or a person, her stinger will stay in the skin of the mammal. Part of her insides will stay there, too. The bee will die.

When our bee is about three weeks old, her hardest job begins. This is when we see her in our world, flying from flower to flower to get nectar. She is now a forager bee. "Forage" means to hunt for food, and that's just what she's doing.

The bee lands on a flower and sucks in nectar through her proboscis, a long, flexible tube on her head. She stores the nectar in her honey stomach. After she's collected as much as she can carry, she flies back to the hive. She shares the nectar with her sisters, who eat some and store the rest in honey cells.

proboscis

In the honey cells, the water in the stored nectar evaporates. The nectar becomes thick. That's the sweet, delicious honey we eat!

A worker bee usually lives for about six weeks in the spring and summer. She gathers nectar for three of those weeks, making about 400 trips altogether. In all those trips, she will collect only enough nectar to make about 7 grams of honey— the size of a packet of sugar.

Our bee also does another very important job while she collects nectar. When she lands on flowers, she gets flower pollen on her hind legs. Some of the pollen she scrapes into pollen baskets to bring back to the hive. The rest of the pollen rubs onto other flowers. Pollen from other flowers helps flowering plants make seeds and new plants.

Our forager bee is done for today. It's time to go back to the hive. She flies straight back—in a

beeline.

Look at all these bees. There are 60,000 bees in this bee colony. Most of them are worker bees doing their jobs.

The next time you see beautiful flowers,
or taste some delicious honey, thank a bee.
And the next time you see a honeybee
flying from flower to flower, remember,
she doesn't want to sting you.

She's too busy!

Dance Like a Honeybee

Honeybees communicate using smell, taste, and touch. Many scientists think they also communicate by doing special dances! When a forager bee finds nectar, she goes back to the hive to tell her sisters where the flowers are. If the flowers are toward the sun, she dances in a kind of figure 8 pattern. If the flowers are to the right of the sun, she runs up the honeycomb toward the right. The faster the bee dances, the closer the food is. Can you communicate with a friend without talking? Here's an experiment for you to try.

Here's what you'll need:

- "nectar" (something sweet, such as a candy bar, an apple, or a box of raisins)
- A friend
- A code (Use the code on the following page or make up your own.)

1. Hide the "nectar" from your friend.

2. Ask your friend to find the "nectar."

3. Help your friend find it—without talking! You can only move your body. Use a code to give clues. Your friend needs to know the code, too.

4. Now have your friend hide the "nectar" for you, and start over.

The Code:

Wiggle your right arm: *go right.*

Wiggle your left arm: *go left.*

Spin around: *go the other way.*

Move your knees up and down: *go upstairs.*

Point down: *go downstairs.*

Run in place very fast: *you're very close.*

Sit down: *you've just passed it.*

Squat down: *look under something.*

Use a mirror to read!

What Did You Discover?

Was it easy or hard to communicate without talking? Unlike bees, people use spoken language to communicate most of the time. But we also do communicate with "body language." We smile, frown, point our fingers. Can you think of other ways people communicate with each other?

WARNING: Honeybees do not sting often, and when they do, the sting is usually painful but not harmful. However, some people (about 4 in a hundred) have bee sting allergies, which can lead to serious distress and even death. The symptoms of an allergic reaction to a bee sting include headache, muscle cramps, fever, drowsiness or unconsciousness, and difficulty with breathing or swallowing. Call 911 immediately if such symptoms are observed. Also be aware that other insects, such as wasps, hornets, or other types of bees, can sting more readily than honeybees. Use caution around all stinging insects.

Neither the publisher nor the author, illustrator, or consultants shall be liable for any injury associated with bee, hornet, or wasp stings following the purchase or use of this book.

To create her paintings, Carla Golembe used gouache on watercolor paper.

Text copyright © 2002 Deborah Heiligman
Illustrations copyright © 2002 Carla Golembe

First paperback printing 2007
ISBN: 978-1-4263-0157-5

Published by the National Geographic Society.

Book design by LeSales Dunworth.
Text is set in Gill Sans. The title type is Bauer Bodoni.

Jump Into Science™ series consultant: Gary Brockman, Early Education Science Specialist
Honeybees expert consultant: Sue Hubbell, beekeeper and author

Library of Congress Cataloging-in-Publication Data
Heiligman, Deborah.
Honeybees/by Deborah Heiligman; illustrated by Carla Golembe.
p. cm. — (Jump into science)
ISBN 0-7922-6678-1 (hardcover)
1. Honeybee—Juvenile literature. [1. Honeybee. 2. Bees.] I. Golembe, Carla, ill. II. Title. III. Series.
QL568.A6 H388 2002
595.79'9—dc21   2001001717

Printed in the United States of America

DEBORAH HEILIGMAN is an award-winning author who has written a number of *Let's-Read-and-Find-Out* books. She's also the author of the New York Public Library's *Kid's Guide to Research.* She's not a beekeeper, although her name "Deborah" means "bee." She lives in New York City. Visit her Web site at www.deborahheiligman.com.

CARLA GOLEMBE is the author-illustrator of a number of books for children. She has received illustration awards from the *New York Times, Parent's Choice,* and the American Folklore Society. She lives in Silver Spring, Maryland. Visit her website at www.carlagolembe.com.

One of the world's largest nonprofit scientific and educational organizations, the National Geographic Society was founded in 1888 "for the increase and diffusion of geographic knowledge." Fulfilling this mission, the Society educates and inspires millions every day through its magazines, books, television programs, videos, maps and atlases, research grants, the National Geographic Bee, teacher workshops, and innovative classroom materials. The Society is supported through membership dues, charitable gifts, and income from the sale of its educational products. This support is vital to National Geographic's mission to increase global understanding and promote conservation of our planet through exploration, research, and education. For more information, please call 1-800-NGS-LINE (647-5463) or write to the following address:

NATIONAL GEOGRAPHIC SOCIETY
1145 17th Street N.W.
Washington, D.C. 20036-4688
U.S.A.
Visit the Society's Web site at www.nationalgeographic.com

Bannockburn School Dist. 106
2165 Telegraph Road
Bannockburn, Illinois 60015